SOMEONE
IS MISSING

Leading Through the Authentic Self

DR. EUGENE KENT AUSTIN II

Trilogy Christian Publishers

A Wholly Owned Subsidiary of Trinity Broadcasting Network

2442 Michelle Drive

Tustin, CA 92780

For information, address Trilogy Christian Publishing

Rights Department, 2442 Michelle Drive, Tustin, CA 92780.

Trilogy Christian Publishing/ TBN and colophon are trademarks of Trinity Broadcasting Network.

For information about special discounts for bulk purchases, please contact Trilogy Christian Publishing.

10 9 8 7 6 5 4 3 2 1

Library of Congress Cataloging-in-Publication Data is available.

ISBN 979-9-89333-034-2

ISBN (ebook) 979-9-89333-035-9

TABLE OF CONTENTS

INTRODUCTION
What Motivated This Book

This book is motivated by an inspiring and liberating moment in which I was reintroduced to the authentic self, Me! The uniquely designed and divinely purposed and ordained person whom God called years ago was missing. It was through God's grace and individuals brave enough in my life to ensure I was reintroduced to the self who was ordained from the time conceived in my mother's womb. In some kind of way, Eugene Kent Austin II was lost under all the titles, degrees, corporate promotions, and societal titles. For years self was lost under the title of Reverend, Pastor, Reverend Dr., Dr., Elder, Evangelist, and I could only imagine my family was asking themselves what ever happened to the individual who was full of laughter, the one who enjoyed dancing, going to the movies, cracking jokes, going out with the family other than for church conferences, retreats, and workshops? The most disturbing discovery was the fact the last one to notice that someone was missing was the one missing...Me!

For years I traveled throughout the United States and overseas doing revivals, workshops, and serving in church administration and it was in my view for the sake of the kingdom. From 1994 to 2009 my life was filled with busyness, including meeting deadlines, driving bishops and pastors to national and state conferences, developing budgets, and attending Seminary, just to name a few. Realize the keyword was "busyness," which I now understand in reflection does not always result in productivity. The quickest response from me was to the title Pastor and I would at times feel insulted or disrespected if someone called me by my first name. Someone was slowly disappearing or dissolving, unbeknownst to me. It was happening so fast because the pace of ministry had become the normal pace of life. The year was measured by church events, state conventions, church anniversaries, and annual workshops. I missed so many pivotal events in my children's lives and once I was reintroduced to the true me, I promised the Lord I would pen my experience and recovery to those who are losing themselves in the busyness of ministry. After years of hesitation and procrastination, I am sitting down in humility and awe of God's grace to grant me this honor to equip those in ministry with tools to build boundaries and strategies to rediscover and reintroduce themselves back into active living toward fullness and wholeness. This is not only for ourselves, but also for those who are on this journey cheering us on along the way.

One needs only to watch the local and national news, stream through social media, or reflect on personal knowledge to find that several senior pastors have committed suicide, many suffer from depression, obesity, high blood pressure, and diabetes, just to name a few. Others of us may be too busy running the church to have a medical examination. Those going through a season of depression are forced to suffer in silence because they feel the environment is not safe to call for help. Pastor Austin is preaching, teaching, praying, visiting the sick, burying loved ones, and meeting church deadlines, but Eugene is suffering each day with nowhere to go and hide, no one to call, and what was my answer whenever my wife would ask, "What's wrong?" My answer was a quick, abrasive, and defensive "Nothing!"

Pastors and leaders within the church are both men and women, so please note that as I refer to my spouse as my wife throughout this book, where the term "wife" is used women could replace this term with "husband." To remain inclusive of my female colleagues the term spouse will be used in place of one's wife or husband.

I thank God for the grace through the bravery of those who loved me enough to speak up, for professors who opened my mind to a new and engaging approach to ministry, and most of all to my family for their patience and determination to hang in there with me until I rediscovered and reintroduced myself back into active participation in this thing called life. As I always say, I have been walking as Pastor Austin for the longest time, but after getting reintroduced to Eugene I like hanging with him so much more. I pray this book and the most intimate experiences shared will help you find that one who is missing: You!

Purpose of This Book

The purpose of this book is to help those in ministry identify areas of emptiness and the feeling of unfulfilled voids in our lives due to fast-paced, overly obligated, and neglected lives smothered in busyness. The testimonies and reflections are provided to assist the readers with identifying danger zones that could lead to seasons of disaster, depression, and even death. This death could be that of a marriage, relationship, ministry, spiritual, mental, or physical.

There are tools provided within this book that may not be an absolute and guaranteed solution; however, applying them to our lives could serve as intentional efforts toward a holistic life. Before we can remove all the clutter under which we are hiding, there must first be an identification of what the clutter is. Not only are there efforts to identify what we have covered, but hidden we should also examine how the pile was dumped on us in the first place. This could be a pile of titles, obligations, disappointments, hurts, our past, or the present. Slowly, our true identity was lost under years of events and experiences that I don't believe God ever purposed for us to become lost under, behind, or underneath.

Once we have identified what caused it and how we became missing, there is the discussion of rediscovery of who we truly are and what we were purposed for. Who is it that we were created to be? What wonderful gifts, talents, and personalities are hidden, missing from the kingdom agenda? Who is it that the world outside of our homes knows? Who do our closest family members, our spouses, and confidants know? Is it really us, or is it the one we want them to know or who they have identified us to be? These questions must be answered: how do I get to know who I truly am? If that is not the person I was created to be, how do I rediscover that person? How do I get reintroduced to that one that has been missing for so long? This is a dedicated effort towards empowering readers to redefine their personhood and rediscover the art of being fully human. Dr. Leo F. Buscaglia emphasizes the importance of your life and the urgency one should have to take advantage of the life you have been blessed with. He provides the thought, "Life is an 'immense journey' and each of us has only one lifetime to travel it. We will wind our own way continuously and relentlessly molding, growing, remodifying our undefined course, performing acts we can never redo on a path we can never retrace."[1]

Reading this book comes at the right time of your life, because you are still alive and your journey is not over. No matter if you traveled for the past two, ten, fifty, or even more years, this is the right time to ensure you don't waste another day merely existing as a bystander without taking control and actively participating in charting out your own journey. There are tools, organizations, support groups, and counseling centers to get us back on track and to help us rediscover ourselves. Let the digging begin.

Finally, it is my desire to walk us through the world of rediscovering not only who we are and are ordained to be, but also redefining our families and how and where we fit into their destiny and dreams. This can't be done without asking the questions: do we need to make amends to those who have been affected during our absence? What are the conversations we need to have with our spouse and our children, and what is the new strategy to ensure there are proactive measures for family wholeness? There were conversations that were very uncomfortable, yet these conversations were much needed to foster healing and restoration for myself, my spouse, our children, and our marriage as a whole.

---

1   Leo F. Buscaglia, *Personhood, The Art of Being Fully Human,* (Fawcett Columbine, New York: Ballentine Books, 1982), 2

There are no shortcuts to this process, and success is not a place or destination but a continuous relational journey. Our children are only children for a short period of time; they will only graduate from high school once, and there is only one last high school event or awards ceremony. What is it that we have missed and how do we make up for the times we were physically, mentally, or emotionally absent due to the busyness of what we called ministry?

Once we have reached the place of rediscovery and we have reintroduced ourselves to the one missing in action all these years, we can chart out the new journey filled with boundaries, fences with gates locked to which only we hold the key. This new journey involves vacations, the respite of which we are fully present in the moment and not distracted by texts and Facebook messages, still connected to the very clutter that overshadowed us in the first place. We will unearth the precious jewel of disconnecting and disengaging for healing, restoration, and spiritual formation. In all that we are facing in the fast paced twenty-first-century society, we must disconnect, and not ask permission to do so. I can only hope and pray that through obedience to the guidance of the Holy Spirit, this book will lead readers into the world of liberation, reinvigorating each relationship one conversation at a time. No false promises are hidden, and there are no quick fixes or shortcuts to this rediscovery and reintroduction of the one who has been missing. Once you rediscover yourself, know that ebbs and flows of life can quickly begin to dump on us, covering us up all over again. Let us begin identifying and removing the clutter piece by piece.

CHAPTER 1
Missing in Action

There was a song sung in many of the services I attended as a small boy entitled "I'm a Soldier in the Army of the Lord" and in this song the words describe a fight for one's life in the Army of the Lord. Well, I have witnessed many soldiers who began fighting in the Army of the Lord who are missing in action. For those who have enlisted in the military or have any knowledge of war, you know that "missing in action" refers to those who were lost in the midst of battle during the war. Nobody found them; those missing in action never returned home, and to this day have not been heard from. They are still listed as active duty, but no one knows their whereabouts. For years I was missing but yet in action. My voice was not the one heard; it was the voices of others, the voices of those who took control of my life, bad doctrine, dehumanizing traditions, the over-extension and over-obligation to going beyond being fully myself which had muted my voice and my authentic identity. This identity was not just who am I, but where I am. What happened to the freedom of being fully and authentically me?

What comes to mind and, amazingly, what is sad is that at least during times of war and conflict, when someone is missing in action their name is written somewhere as a part of history; there are memorial services to commemorate and honor those yet missing in action. My wife and I took our children to visit the Vietnam Memorial Wall and it held the names of those who were lost during the war. It was interesting to note that there were attendants who ensured you did not lean on the wall or walk in certain areas to honor the wall that bears the names of those who gave the ultimate sacrifice. How much more should there be attention given to those who are operating in ministry, CEOs of Fortune 500 companies, business owners, pastors, and their families who are busy with day-to-day tasks, meeting deadlines and fulfilling obligations, but who are void and empty, with nothing left? It is almost as if they are operating on automatic as in the movie *Get Out,* directed by Jordan Peele, functioning but empty within the shell of our exhausted and drained bodies. We are very active but unengaged, or rather disengaged. This is a time to take what we call a strategic pause to do a self-examination in answering the following questions honestly to evaluate our status and to find out if we are missing in action:

1. Is your idea of a vacation or getaway attending a church, religious, work-related conference, workshop, convention, or retreat?

     ____Yes ____No

2. You often feel guilty for taking time off from your job, pulpit, or business?

     ____Yes ____No

3. Leaving my phone in the car or at home causes anxiousness and anxiety.

     ____Yes ____No

4. Spending time with my family, loved ones or friends outside of church-related, business-related environments feels awkward.

     ____Yes ____No

5. Focusing on the conversation at hand is difficult because thoughts of my obligations and office responsibilities distract me.

     ____Yes ____No

6. Someone calling me by my first name rather than by my title or position seems foreign or upsets me, making me feel uncomfortable.

    ____Yes ____No

7. My marriage or relationships are less fulfilling than when I am operating or involved in my occupation or calling.

    ____Yes ____No

8. Going to a church meeting or keeping a counseling appointment with a parishioner or business partner is more important than attending my family members' engagements, and events.

    ____Yes ____No

9. I am committed to setting dates and uninterrupted time with my family as a standing appointment.

    ____Yes ____No

10. Do you have an annual physical examination and know who your family physician is?

    ____Yes ____No

How did you score? This questionnaire has no calculating scale; it is merely a tool to provoke reflection and authentic coming to grips with if we are truly missing in action, or in other words, merely functioning. Has dysfunction become normal operation for us? We owe it to ourselves to be fully engaged, involved, and active in our own lives. No one should have more participation in our lives than the one whowas created to live it out. You are worth it, and important enough for a wake-up call. Time is going faster and faster each year, and it waits for no one. A note of encouragement concerning this evaluation: it should not be a tool to drive you further into despair or guilt but should be used only as a tool of reflection and to bring forth awareness that we may need to make some changes in our lives, ministries, and/or professions.

If you have gone through this evaluation and realized some areas that need attention and you ignore the signs, it is only a matter of time before the walls come crumbling down. It may not be today, maybe not tomorrow, next year, or the next, but rest assured there is going to be a breakdown somewhere; hopefully and prayerfully there is room for recovery.

Continuing to reference soldiers missing in action, at least there is a search party that is sent out to perform recon to rescue our lost loved ones; even today there are searches in Vietnam for those who were lost in action, prisoners of war. If not for the individuals themselves, there is hope to at least recover their remains. How much more so would it seem fitting to send out search teams for those who are suffering in ministry, or maybe just existing, void of being? We can gain a high off being over-extended to obligations, and the more we pile on our plate the more sense of spirituality and closeness to fulfillment we can have. It can even be addictive, as overwhelming as it may be. From my own personal experience, it seemed as though the more I piled on, the more ministry stress I was under, the more the Lord was pleased. How wrong and off I was. This was a total misconception of what God's purpose was for my life. One of the things I lacked most was balance. This is a keyword for ministry success, "balance." This is not a state or end, but a continuous balancing of family, physical, spiritual, mental, financial, and professional elements. Oh yeah, I almost forgot; these are not important because we are not present enough to grant ourselves permission to take control of the intentional balancing of our lives. We are too presupposed to await others' approval of the taking control of our lives...of course, we need their approval and permission? Wrong!

CHAPTER 1

How Did It Happen?

Before we can relocate ourselves, we must take time to truly journey through the areas of neglect and ignoring of the self. Let's look at the areas of the questionnaire as well as possible reasons for our absence. In reflection, you may find that no one may have even known you went missing, possibly because they never were introduced to the authentic you beyond titles and positions. Either way, we can only hope and pray that the alarm has gone off and there is a wake-up call.

CHAPTER 2
Following the Evidence

Having presented in general this book's approach toward enlightening leaders about what it means to have gone missing, we can go into further details. Not only should we be aware of the signs and clues, but we should also examine and understand other things that could come with our subconscious absence. One caught up in leading in the fast paced, social media-driven, corporate structure of this twenty-first century should note that as we are missing in action, those we serve may not even realize or care that we are operating on automatic.

Depending on how you responded to this questionnaire, I thought it needful to examine not only what you answered but also the contributing factors connected to these "Yes" or "No" responses. The fact is that when a person goes missing, if we look closely enough we will find some sort of evidence as to what happened. Take a look at the evidence resonating from your questionnaire responses. Question number one is formulated to dig into what is referred to as respite. This is the time one should plan as a standing date to get away from and disconnect from the day-to-day hustle and bustle involved with your vocation or calling. For many years my idea of vacations for my family was our attendance at church conventions, workshops, or temporary duty assignments (TDY) for my corporate job. This was not healthy at all, simply because although physically we were in the same geographic location, there was no true interaction or relational engagement. While my wife was attending to the children and getting them ready for the morning sessions, I was away in meetings or preparing the conference rooms for the daytime sessions. My wife was with the children at the pool and I was at the airport picking up a guest speaker or going to the local Walmart to pick up needed supplies for the night activities. By the way, being that I was missing in action, I was not aware of the fact my wife was frustrated with carrying the load of getting the children dressed to attend the different events for the day, and I was also not aware of her exhaustion from staying up all night waiting for my return to the room and getting up early in the morning. She continued to do what was needed to ensure the children got what they needed.

What is your idea of a vacation and why? Take into consideration your spouse's idea of a getaway. Have you discussed with your family their idea of a vacation? You may even find having family discussions of when and where you will take vacation could be enjoyable for the entire family. If you are unable to answer this question because you don't have time to think about vacation or just don't consider a vacation, this is a clue that someone is missing but still in action. Kirk Byron Jones's *Rest in the Storm* is a great book for every leader to read. It is his personal testimony of how leading a congregation that was healthy, thriving, and expanding and the lack of respite resulted in his collapse physically, mentally, and spiritually. Dr. Jones introduces the theological example of Jesus' intentional journey to the hinder parts of the ship to do nothing else but sleep. Even after reading his book and meeting him personally while I attended Samuel Dewitt Proctor School of Divinity, it would take my own collapse to bring me to grips with ensuring I scheduled time away from the fast pace of my corporate and religious responsibilities. What evidence is left from your response to this question? What are the clues and evidence of your inability to answer this question?

What would you say to those who ignore the evidence or proof? During Kirk Byron Jones' lecture, he was postured on the stage and I could still remember the brilliance of his delivery and the intentional pauses within each stanza of his delivery. It was almost as if he was giving the audience the opportunity not only to ponder his points but also to respond. Lo and behold while he was describing Jesus' intentional efforts to journey to the back of the boat, there was a student sitting right in front of me who whispered, "I will get plenty of time to rest when I am dead." It was right then Dr. Jones seemingly adjusted his lecture to include the response as he looked in the direction of the whisper "Sooner than later!" Wow, you could hear a pin drop in the room. It was a lecture I would never forget. It was during my own collapse, while on my bed of affliction, depressed, unable to even get up and use the restroom, that I opened the book a second time and the Lord granted me *Rest in the Storm* of my life. So again, what is the evidence lingering around your response to the first question?

Question two is focused on your ability to internalize your feelings concerning not just getting away but merely taking time off from the job. There is a minimal cost for taking time off, especially when you have vacation days accrued. How do you feel when you take time off from the job, away from the pulpit, away from serving in your local church? Is there a sense of guilt because you think you let the company, church, people, or even God down because of the urgency and survival of all things predicated upon your uninterrupted presence and involvement? Remember that Jesus Himself took time away, and there is no evidence of Him repenting and feeling guilty for doing so. What is making you feel guilty about intentional self-care? What makes us attend events, and obligations even when they can be detrimental to our physical, spiritual, and mental health? I have coined the term "Ever Ready Rigor" because of the Energizer Bunny's continuously moving and functioning as if to think we have this unrealistic belief of our ability to keep going and going and going without any rest or even looking at what is in front of us. What is causing you to feel guilty about taking much-needed time off? If you checked "No," you have to be careful of that as well. There are times when we have scheduled events within the church and it requires our presence and accountability as leaders, chief executive officers (CEO), or business owners and we don't want to neglect our responsibilities. However, this time off ensures we are operating on all cylinders and attentive.

Question three is one befitting this information-aged, social media-driven generation. The cell phone has become an extension of our bodies and selves. It is almost as if we are more concerned with losing our cell phones than remembering to take our medication with us. What is important is where our focus resides. Where is your treasure laid up and where is your focus? Imagine going into a restaurant and all of a sudden remembering you have left your phone in the car. How are you feeling right now? Have you left your party in the restaurant and anxiously run out to the car to retrieve your cell phone? Are you at the table with family and friends picking up your phone to check voicemails, Facebook messages, texts, or status updates? What is the evidence or clues left of your physical presence but your attention is far from engagement with those closest to you? You are physically present but missing from the moment. This leads to question four.

How do you feel when you have alone time with your family? Do conversations with family or significant others feel awkward or make you feel uncomfortable? Do you find conversations with coworkers, co-laborers, or friends outside of your family more comfortable and entertaining than those with your spouse, children, or other family members? How you responded to this question, especially answering it honestly, serves as proof of our absence consciously. It could be in response to the fact that we are not used to having open and honest conversations with those physically closest to us. What are the ingredients raising the levels of anxiety during conversations with our spouses, children, and parents? What is it we are anxiously anticipating that will arise during the conversations?

In times past I found conversations with those at church, on my job, and visiting with other couples more engaging and open than those within the confines of conversational dialogue with my wife. What was it that built a wall, a gulf, between the one that was most supportive and loving to me? Why was I finding myself defensive in anticipation that the next statement or question was going to uncover some hidden compartment of criticism, correction, or reveal a trait of imperfection?

Upon events that would unfold, which I will discuss in a later chapter, I discovered that much of what I was experiencing was a direct result of the fact that I had become immune to inauthentic conversations with those who were not as intimate and close to me as those within my home. My wife knew the real me, while others became acquainted with the inauthentic me. They knew Dr. Austin, Dr. A, Reverend Doctor Austin, the pastor, the evangelist, the information technology specialist, they knew the professor of a prominent theological seminary; however, my wife knew the real me. It was evident I was not prepared to discuss the real me, the one who was suffering from past hurts, childhood issues, addictions, depression, and insecurities, and her grace and her spiritual ability to love and to cover me permitted me to go missing and hide under all of the different titles and positions I had accomplished and achieved. However, how long could I go missing and how long could I hide from the truth of where I was headed? One could only hope I could come out of hiding or be discovered before it was too late.

How is the conversation with your children? Are your children able to engage in conversation with their parents, or are they engaged in conversation with their pastor? One of the thoughts I received while preparing to have a life-changing conversation with one of my children was "Your child does not need to talk to the pastor; they need their father." Wow! The Spirit of the Lord convicted me that I was missing all those years and my children were missing their father and speaking to the pastor, hidden behind all of the super-spiritual jargon that is most common to those raised and operating in the twentieth and twenty-first-century churches and nonprofit organizations. One of the reasons for hiding behind the sacred office and not engaging in intimate and revealing conversations with our children could be the fact that we are not ready to hear what is truly going on in the minds and hearts of our children. I had become accustomed to hiding under the title and position rather than the divine and most honorable calling, to be a full and human father to our children and most of all husband of my wonderful wife. Not only was I missing from them, but I was as well missing the full experience of a life of discovery of who these special and gifted individuals truly were as wonderfully and beautifully created individuals. Question to every reader: what are you missing out on during your absence? What are you missing out on while missing in action? Only you can openly and honestly answer these questions.

CHAPTER 3
Hidden Under All the Yeses

We can find ourselves totally disengaged from conversations simply because subconsciously we have checked out, focusing on the next big task awaiting us. I can remember numerous times when my wife was telling me about her day and although I was there physically, my mind wandered onward and out to what happened at the office or what great task was awaiting me the next day. During her sharing of the events that unfolded during the day, she would ask me, "Are you listening to me?" and of course, my response would be "Yeah, love, I am listening." This answer was not given fully under false pretenses, because I was listening, although in the forefront of my mind were all the daunting tasks facing me the next day as a result of all of the yeses I had promised. My life had become a mountain of over-obligation and anxiousness to continuously respond to every request with a yes. No matter how tired I was or how frustrated I became, there was the loss of the ability to say that one word... "No"! Even when individuals would not directly request anything from me, I would volunteer my talents, gifts, and abilities to help. Yes, I can go and pick up. Yes, I will come and preach. Yes, I can go TDY to Florida, and Yes, I can make the meeting. Well, to put it another way, as I was telling everyone else yes, I was telling my family no, or "I will get to you when I am not tired and frustrated from all of the yeses already promised to everyone else." To my family, I was hidden under all the yeses. I was not only missing from my family, but all the yeses smothered my existence. Who was looking back at me when I looked in the mirror?

There can be several causes as to why we are prone to say yes to every request. How conscious are you and how present are you while engaged in conversations? Are your thoughts overwhelmed with keeping track of all the yeses you offered? This task alone can be overwhelming if you don't have a calendar to keep a schedule of your obligations. Take this time to reflect on your current schedule, how you track your obligations, who you commit to, what you commit to, and the boundaries you currently have protecting the time and space set aside for yourself and your family. Take time to reflect over and internalize your current feelings right now.

We need to note the reasoning behind our inability to say no! Why is it that we cannot say no to individuals who may not have our best interest at heart, but those who care the most for us hear the "no response" more often verbally and nonverbally due to our non-response or absence? How long will you be able to function with over-obligation and how long will it be until all the yeses smother you to death? You can only be covered for so long before it chokes the life out of you. Time for you to come up for air after being smothered by all the yeses you have delivered throughout your week to make room by simply saying no. The more you say it the more comfortable you will feel. I used to hear the saying "practice makes perfect" but I will beg to differ. "Perfect practice makes perfect"; in other words, how you practice is how you perform. Practice saying "No!" intentionally like you truly mean it. Say it and deliver it with enthusiasm.

The load will be removed one response at a time. One of the ways that CEOs, leaders, pastors, and managers are missing from their true purpose is due to the fact there is an over- obligation to nonproductive ventures and projects. A good approach is to ask questions about the overall objective attached to the task requested. It is okay to ask "Why?" In the event your asking why is too much for those requesting actions from you, then one would be moved in curiosity to the motive behind the request in the first place. Much of our frustration at home could be due to all of the yeses and smiles we delivered on the other side of the threshold.

As we begin to remove the piles of yeses smothering us and covering up our authentic person, we will surely find ourselves more present within the current conversations we are engaged in. Honestly, now when my wife is sharing her thoughts and experiences with me I find myself more often in awe at her revelations and discoveries and I believe it is a direct result of my view being clear of all of the yeses that previously covered my conscious presence. I am now actively listening without thinking of what I am going to prepare for my response or what my next word is going to be. The anxiety is quieting down, and I am actively and intentionally engaging in every word, phrase, and narrative presented by my children, my spouse, and those who are important enough to have my full attention. There is a more protected area of our lives that must remain constant and an intentional act is to ensure there are boundaries. This boundary is reinforced through the response of "No," "Wait" or "I can't fulfill that obligation at this time." This comes with a clear understanding of the contexts in which we serve. This is going to take time for yourself and those who have become dependent upon your deliverables. Reverend Luis A. Carrier, Pastor of Everette Free Methodist Church, discussed how leaders and congregants often misinterpret boundaries "as the leaders not being nice, or rude."[2] Arriving at this place takes self-liberation beyond the misconceptions of those looking to suck the life out of you and to erase your existence of who God ordained you to be under the fake smiles offered simply to pacify those who care nothing of your self-balance nor the authentic you. This does little for the relationship and makes one uncomfortable for all parties because the very sense of ministry is immersed in authentic spiritual intimacy. I'm not one to intrude into your life, but if this is you, I humbly and with all urgency implore you to begin to remove the pile of yeses by building boundaries one at a time. Let the building begin.

---

2   Marie Fortune, *Priestly Ministry and Healthy Boundaries: Freedom Through Boundaries.* (Chicago: The National Organization for Continuing Education of Roman Catholic Clergy, Inc., 1997).

CHAPTER 4

Building Boundaries for All

While building boundaries is healthy and liberating for the individual, it is most healthy and helpful in protecting the self of those whom we serve as well. Rabbi Julie S. Schwartz, Temple Emanu-El, explains how "boundaries make it safe in relationships and let me know who I am versus who you are. Boundaries allow me to keep being me without merging into who you are."[3] This can reveal a very liberating act and love for not only ourselves but those whom we serve. Never do we want to hijack others' moments of authenticity by bleeding all over who the Lord purposed for them to be, nor do we want others intruding in or bleeding all over who we are purposed to be. Once the boundaries are placed, they should not be relaxed for any reason. Remember, the boundaries were placed there for a reason. No matter how close we may feel to others, boundaries should remain in place for the protection of all.

Marie Fortune explains the importance of relational boundaries for all in the lives of twenty-first century leaders:

- They help us maintain clear professional relationships.
- They are guidelines (usually unwritten) that help us know when and when not to participate in a given activity, especially if we have more power.
- They are not intended to shackle us but to free us in our work as spiritual leaders.
- They help us keep perspective when people's problems seem overwhelming.
- They signal to others that it is safe to trust us.
- They protect congregants/students from our abuse of power. Our power is derived from our education, our

---

3   Ibid.

position as spiritual leaders, and our resources. The very act of ordination sets us apart as having more power and designates us for leadership.[4]

Boundaries, again, ensure the safety and continued professionalism of those who are called to serve and those to whom we serve. Organizations, professionals, ministers, educators, and others serving in human services operating continuously without boundaries create unhealthy practices, unhealthy individuals, and unhealthy environments which will eventually result in unhealthy organizations. It is only a matter of time before collateral damage begins to unfold.

I take a pause to discuss the current issues we face with the lack of boundaries within social media. It has opened our world up to a different spectrum. The ability to connect through messaging, Facebook, Instagram, Snapchat, and Twitter is endless. Marie Fortune continues with ensuring leaders are aware:

> Spiritual leadership is replete with boundary challenges. Often the lines between what is appropriate and what is not are unclear. In addition, most of us struggle with ambivalence about boundaries and about the power and authority that we hold as faith leaders. Even as we may have come to some awareness about the basics of healthy boundaries, the issues before us get more complex every day. Internet technology and social media have added a whole new layer of complexity to boundary issues. Our ethical bottom line is to question whether a boundary crossing is in the best interest of the congregant and the congregation.[5]

The continuous question in front of every action we can take is how is what I'm about to do going to affect myself and those

---

4   Ibid, 7.
5   Ibid.

around me as well as the connected communities? What are the boundaries that you practice with social media and have you discussed this with your significant other or your children? One of the discussions between my wife and me is the boundaries and practices we have within social media. These are practices that are agreed upon between the two of us and may not be applicable to other families. You have to be conscious of the inner alarms triggering the moment when correspondence crosses boundaries. In the event you are married and you receive an instant message from the opposite sex, are you able to share the message with your spouse? Again, this is the beginning of what Dr. James Harris calls "bifurcated" in that we are spiritual in public but we branch off into a different, hidden character behind closed doors. Who are we after the benediction? Someone is missing, and it is the real us. To reaffirm the importance of boundaries, there is often some gray area when there is no clear definition of a requirement or its importance in terms of setting boundaries. However, without these boundaries, clergy members, leaders, CEOs, and their communities remain at risk of unethical and unprofessional relationships. Boundaries are better for all parties.

CHAPTER 5

Stolen Identity

In trying to keep up with this fast paced, social media-driven world it is easy to lose ourselves and who we are called to be. Within this chapter, we are called to take a good look at our current identity. How do you identify yourself? Take a moment to see yourself today. Who am I and how did I get to this place of identity? Consider the offices you hold, your occupation, your hobbies, your marital status, your children, and your circles. Am I identifying myself with who God has ordained and called me to be as an individual, or do I identify myself with what I do or my gifts talents and abilities? If I am not seeing myself as a wonderful and beautiful God-made individual, then possibly my identity has been stolen. One of the questions digs into our response to what people call us. This is a good time to take a few moments to journal how you currently see yourself and your identity by utilizing the following questions to formulate your answers:

1. Who am I?
2. What is the one word that would describe me?
3. I am most critical of the way I_____.
4. How do I feel about others' opinions of me?
5. If I could change one thing about myself, I would change _____.
6. How do I introduce myself to people when we first meet, by title or name?

Identity Theft

In the cyber world, there is an increase in identity theft. This is described as individuals using tools, software, and methods of acquiring your identity to commit crimes, erase their crimes, or gain access to your private information. It is like gaining access to your life and taking control of certain areas to fit their agenda. Just looking at the news and different televised programs or articles, you will find individuals who have experienced their identity being stolen, resulting in criminals ordering credit cards, taking out loans, and having their personal accounts hacked, leaving the victims in mounting debt. In some way, the imposters were able to gain unauthorized access into the lives of victims and at times without them even noticing their entire lives have been infiltrated. Their identity is stolen. In some instances there is not much effort required because victims leave private information lying around or unguarded. Their information is left wide open for the taking.

When we leave ourselves unguarded or we are too accessible, with no boundaries, we are vulnerable to intruders stealing our identity. In other words, people will begin to place labels on us and we are no longer viewed as authentic beings or our individual selves. We simply are now labeled by others and take on an identity of how others view us or desire us to be. There was a time I could only identify myself through the titles and positions I held corporately as well as religiously. It was almost as if Eugene K. Austin II was not enough. I was morphed into being referred to as "Dr. Austin," "Dr. A," "Reverend Austin," and "Elder Austin," and to call me by any other name was regarded as demeaning and at times disrespectful. How did I arrive at this point in life and why was being the original and uniquely designed self not enough? Could it be I struggled with even knowing and defining who I was in the first place? In some way, my identity was stolen and I was now walking in what others expected me to be, do, and deliver rather than who I was created to be before I was ever born.

It is easy in the fast-paced calling to ministry and leadership to rarely make time for reflection and self-evaluation of where we are or who we are. As we interact with our children, are we relating to them from our professional position or are we communicating with them as their parents? There are several tools available that could help leaders do self-evaluations that will give us an idea of where we are right now. Self-reflections and journaling can enable us to examine not only where we are at this time in our lives but also how we feel about ourselves. It is through reflection one may be able to identify possible causes and contributors to how we currently feel about where we are in life. One important requirement and necessity is time for reflection. Leaders must make time for reflection. How do you feel when people call you by your first name, title, or position? Why are you feeling a certain way, or is it that you are in a place in ministry that you honestly can't define? Again, someone is missing. Someone missing could be the result of living out the myths others developed and presented in our lives. Edward Wimberly explains leaders have a tendency to live out their lives according to others' truths and views of them. He further notes "... myths refers to the way beliefs and convictions are constructed and how these constructions shape our lives and our behaviors. Beliefs and convictions are represented by certain repetitive themes that appear in the stories we tell."[6] It is possible for us to become engrossed with how others define us. As these stories continue to be told to us day after day, they become the themes of our lives. Conviction sets in from what has been constructed around us. Seems as if there is a sense of obligation to live up to others' expectations. I am all smiles as I walk through the halls of the offices where I serve; however, there could be tears flowing out of my heart. This could all be the result of living out a life constructed by what others think of me or how they have defined me. Truly, this is a place of stolen identity.

Within this life and the desire for one to be accepted and affirmed, rarely can one muster up the courage to strip themselves of the religious/professional titles, names and views of what others desire them to live up to. As I reflect on my life and experiences, there are a few areas I can see curve how I defined

---

6   Edward P. Wimberly, *Recalling Our Own Stories, Spiritual Renewal for Religious Caregivers* (San Francisco, CA: Jossey Bass Publishing, 1997), 4

myself. One of the areas at the forefront is culturally/contextually developed identity. This is identity developed and cultivated by the culture or context one's experiences are derived from. In other words, family culture, occupational context, ministry culture, or community culture can cultivate and develop how we view ourselves. How did my family view me, what are the expectations on my job, what is expected of me from my friends, and how do my friends view me? All of this could begin to strip us of our identity as we begin to take on the identity of what others say about us. I am slowly beginning to be stripped of my identity as I am morphed into others' expectations and views of me.

Another area that affected my self-worth and how I viewed myself was my childhood culturally defined identity. Growing up being continuously bullied, in my opinion, cultivated a sense of insecurity and low self-worth. The continuous insults concerning my weight followed me into adulthood, during which I struggled with insecurities and a deep-rooted complex concerning my weight and appearance. I was no longer a self-confident, excited, and outgoing child; I carried a complex which made me closely guarded. I rarely opened myself up to others, fearing I would be judged. My defense mechanism was to beat others to the punch with self-insults and/or crack jokes to make others laugh to minimize the opportunity for others to ridicule me. Some of this defense mechanism is still evident today. I am continuously digging under the past culturally/contextually defined self to get to who Eugene K. Austin II truly is. In all of this, as I come to the reality of a stolen identity, it is easy to see how quickly we can get lost in how others have defined us and their expectations of us.

Finally, as I view my family dynamics coming from divorced parents and then becoming a child within a blended family, it is evident how I began to define myself by what I have been through, my experiences, and the disappointments that I buried under a culturally/contextually defined identity. Others have spoken into my life statements such as "You are going to be just like your daddy!" or "You are never going to be anything because you were born in the town where no one good comes from," just to name a few comments. It was almost as if the voices, although heard over 40 years ago, still remain fresh in my head, replaying over and over again. Underneath is a wonderfully drafted and divinely designed being...Me! I have to find a way to take back my identity. The blessing is I have come to the realization that I am robbing myself of being fully and totally me. I am also robbing the world of meeting the truly authentic being God created me to be.

This, again, is another opportunity for you to reflect back over your life and review past experiences, people, and voices resonating in your head, continuing to rehearse in your ears, robbing and overshadowing who you truly and authentically are. Are you living according to what others defined you to be? Are you a reflection of the home you came from? What negative experiences are overshadowing the light of your destiny today? Whatever it is, whoever it is, no one is more important than who God fearfully and wonderfully created you to be. It will not be easy, but somehow we have to find a way to dig through the past experiences covering up who we are truly called to be. If it is a painstaking struggle, then we must ask ourselves why, and how we take power or authority. I stress, as others are awaiting your gift and what you bring to ministry, we have to find a way to take back our identity.

CHAPTER 6
Taking Back our Identity

There are a few questions to consider at this time. The first question to consider is what is the working definition of identity as it relates to this book? Secondly, what authoritative source empowers and ordains you to take back your identity? In other words, what do the scriptures provide as God's plan for one to live authentically in life and as it relates to ministry and calling? As we are searching for clarity of the Lord's calling on our life, what is the price paid for us living as anyone else but the authentic You? For this book and throughout each chapter, identity is the authentically lived out, divinely designed, and purposed holistically balanced you. It is the inner called being of which God refers to as the whole person living out the ordained purpose and divinely designed being. It is pivotal to the calling and purpose of your life that you live it out as the person God has called and birthed you to be.

One must dig deep within, with great courage and boldness, to examine one's current identification or how one identifies at this time in their life. Webster defines identification as "The act of identifying or state of being identified and proof of identity."[7] This effort is not a one-time act; you must ensure that you are perpetually taking inventory of who you are and where you currently are in life. This is an intentional examination throughout the different stages of life. Life delivers differently and we experience transitional seasons in our lives that shape who we are and become. For we were, we are, and we shall become who the Lord has designed and divinely authored us to be. This is why it is so important that we endeavor to take back our identity. Bruce Wilkinson, in his book *You Were Born For This,* sheds light on the difference between living authentically versus living in light

7   Houghton Mifflin Harcourt, *Websters New Basic Dictionary, Office Edition* (Houghton Mifflin Harcourt Publishing Company, 222 Berkeley Street, Boston, Mass, 2007)

of what others desire you to be. It is the difference between "being forced to choose between...something good and something miraculous."[8] In regards to others experiencing the authentic self and our calling it would be just as others merely experiencing that which is the "good" versus that which is divinely ordained as the "miraculous self." Especially during this pandemic-laden time, the world and they that dwell within are seeking the miraculous. What is an experience of life and what is a transformational experience? When we speak of transformational, it is from a holistic perspective, that which transforms the whole being, spiritually, physically, and psychologically. Yes! You are that important to the equation. This is why it is so important that you get to the root of who you are and if it is lining up with who the Master has ordained you to be. Again I emphasize without apology that you are that important, the one who is crying out underneath all the layers of pleasing others, underneath all of the covers thrown upon the authentic being to smother who you truly are. I can only pray that the flame is beginning to flicker to burn within to take back your identity.

The second question offered for examination within this chapter is what God provides within the Holy Scriptures that speaks to and empowers us. What authority do we stand upon to answer the call and mandate to take back what is rightfully ours, our identity?

For this book, we can look at a working definition as it will relate to the term identity. So what does it look like to invite the one that has been missing all these years? What will it take to give you the courage to welcome the authentic you back into living life to the fullest, authentically? There are books, Ted Talks, podcasts, and workshops today giving tips, tools and strategies; however, what pushes us beyond the last session of a workshop into action? I have often wondered why I remained in bondage so long, living up to expectations and approval of others. Think about that for a

---

8   Bruce Wilkinson, *You Were Born for this: 7 Keys to a Life of Predictable Miracles,* (Multnomah Books Publishing: 12265 Oracle Boulevard, Suite 200, Colorado Springs, Colorado 80921, 2009, p. 68)

moment, what it feels like to have to respond to the calls of others, bound into their deadlines, programs, and standards. What about what your desire, your schedule, your appointments? What has God destined for your life? Wow! You mean to tell me that it is all right for me to ponder the Lord's desires for my life? This is the initial takeoff towards freedom and liberty to roll out the red carpet for that special guest arriving shortly.

It is the initial entrance into that breath of fresh air, breathing in the newness and freshness of my very own thoughts and desires. This is to be done without apology or reservation. It is possibly through reflection on your history or past that you can begin to uncover all the pressure or historical rubbish that's been covering the door closing out the authentic you. To ensure this read does not highjack your moment, the quest begins with your own personal journey through your past, although there is no model tailored to fit all simply because no one is the same. We are all unique; however, there are a few thoughts to consider as you reflect on your own past and history. Consider the following:

1. Where did I come from, what city, state, country?

2. What are my family dynamics?

3. What pivotal events and experiences shaped, traumatically, dramatically, positively or negatively affected my life?

4. Do I know my family history beyond my grandparents?

5. How were my spiritual or theological beliefs shaped?

6. What financial principles were taught to me?

7. How was I introduced into sexuality; what were my initial sexual experiences?

8. What relational values were instilled in me?

9. Did I experience vacations, respite, life outside of the faith community?

10. What was the emphasis on psychological, emotional, mental intelligence/health?

My wonderful wife, whom I will talk about later in this book, introduced me to journaling earlier in our marriage. It is also interesting how, in the first few years of marriage, when I was not open to conversation and discussion, she would write me a letter. The power of writing out your thoughts is transformational. Reflecting back, it puts a smile on my face and I can feel an internal giggling, remembering how when I would shut down she would place a letter on my pillow and how I would melt down the my outer shell as her words would jump off the pages, piercing the core of my heart. Her written words would reach beyond my stubbornness into rationalization of how wrong I was in so many situations. Journaling took me even further into transformational reflection. Not only was my journaling an opportunity for me to talk with God, but also with myself, my past, my present and an opportunity for God to talk to and through me. It is through journaling that you can begin to write down and reflect upon the previously provided questions. Before you invite yourself back into your living, take time to get to know who you truly are through who you were.

Where Did I Come From?

Introducing this question as it relates to journaling, it is important for you to consider the area of the country you come from, the culture, beliefs, family dynamics. Chances are this is a part of what has shaped you. I can remember growing up in Farrell, Pennsylvania, which was a blue-collar city. The majority of my relatives, including my father, worked in the steel mill, so you can only imagine I was part of the great shutdown of all the mills. The people from my hometown are tough, thick-skinned, and at times harsh individuals. We all walked up the hills in the snow during winter and in the heat of the day during the summer to school, and there were very few days that I can remember that school was cancelled due to weather. This could possibly answer why I am quick to respond, at times defensive, or suspect to so many things. Those who grew up in the city streets of Farrell had to fight daily, whether on the playgrounds, to keep lunch money, or simply to defend your reputation. the point is, reflecting on where I grew up now answers so many questions of who the authentic me truly has been and is becoming.

Family Dynamics?

Family dynamics differ in so many ways. Not to get too much into statistics; however, it would be interesting to examine the current dynamics in the world today as it relates to divorcees, single, married, spiritual, employed, LGBTQIA+. Where do you, as a reader, fall in? What are your family dynamics? Did you come from a single-parent home, were your parents married, divorced, did one of your parents die when you were younger? Might be time to take a journaling break. To share my experience, initially my parents were married. However, upon the closing of the steel mill and the depression in my town, my parents divorced when I was about nine years old. At that time, it was only my one sister and me. Things dramatically changed, as I remember my dad coming home one day looking distraught that he no longer had a job at the steel mill. It was only a matter of time, and due to other contributing factors, my parents divorced. To this day, at the age of fifty, I can remember sitting on the steps with my father hearing him tell me he would no longer be living with us and he and my mother would be divorcing. It is interesting to note that I can still remember the color of the wallpaper, the designs speckled throughout it. It was the experience that transcended my childhood, and it is what has developed and shaped who I am today, the authentic me. It would be a few years later that my mother would remarry and from that would be the birth of my second sister. The dynamics continued to change, shaping who I was becoming, how I would view marriage, relationships, communication. It was developing quickly, and at times it seemed I had no control over the events that were unfolding. There were other discoveries I experienced beyond my parents that would have even further effects on my being.

At the age of twelve, I found out that I had a whole other set of relatives that I never knew existed. Wait a minute, God! My world is turning upside down and at the same time there is much joy and anguish occurring at the same time. Go ahead, I will grant you a few days to continue journaling your family history and dynamics. You owe it to yourself, because I assure you God is going to uncover a part of you that possibly has been ignored for far too long. Not only were there blood relatives introduced into my life, the experience would also include siblings from my stepfather's side. The family dynamics become really interesting when you mix in siblings from all sides, which include the relationship between my younger sister from my mother and stepfather's marriage. This is not to say I love her any less; however, the dynamics are different and I am always considering the dynamics of her relationship with her siblings on her father's side. It has a direct impact on who I have become and am becoming to ensure I am relational with her as well as my other sister in a healthy and considerate approach. It is who I am! The question is, am I being authentic and truthful to the history of the family? What about you as you are reflecting on your family dynamics historically?

Pivotal Experiences

This is a time where the emotions may stir, because this is a call to invite you back into areas of your past or even present that were pivotal moments in your life. In this book, when we speak of pivotal it relates to critical, crucial events that have taken place in your life. Maybe there were experiences that served as turning points in your life or even a point where life shut down, or worse, you shut down or shut out everyone. Personally, there were traumatic points in my life that I will never forget. One experience I can remember growing up was when my grandfather suffered a stroke. To see him one day speaking with me and riding around in his blue car with the engine ticking and then the very next day going up to the hospital room and he can barely respond to me... This was one of the first traumatic experiences, not only for me but for my entire family. Seeing my entire family taking up almost the whole floor of the hospital and the emotions years later still stir emotions.

The second traumatic experience was receiving the news that my uncle, who was my hero growing up, had unexpectedly passed away. I remember driving up to North Carolina from Florida for a military temporary duty assignment and stopping off in Georgia overnight. Interestingly, I had a dream that someone close to me had passed away and the dream felt so real. The next morning, I woke up and continued my travel from Georgia to North Carolina and upon checking into the hotel, my commander and the chaplain entered my room to notify me that my uncle had passed away. This rocked my family to the core. This was one of the hardest things I had ever experienced. As I look at his child today, he walks exactly like his father. His child was only a few months old when he passed away. Now he's a grown, successful adult. I can only imagine how proud my uncle would have been of his child.

There were positive experiences, pivotal moments, as well. During my sophomore year in high school, I was the recipient of an invitation to the Hugh Obrian Leadership conference at Mount Union College. Being selected from all my peers as the only representative gave me a sense of pride. It was especially notable because my high school was predominantly white, so I was quite honored. Walking in the auditorium filled with thousands of high school sophomores from across the state of Ohio and I was one of the select put in me a sense of confidence that previously I did not have. I remember now that my parents were unable to take me to the conference and one of my tutors drove me all the way to Mount Union. She did not have to do that, and I wish I could remember her name and send her or her family a thank you card some 40 plus years later.

If we are to minister from the authentic self, then we have to truly reflect upon who we are. Who are you? Just as the God had the teacher to drive me to the conference, what earthly angels did God have in place during those pivotal moments of your life?

Your Family Tree

In 2022 our family, after a four-year hiatus due to COVID19, was blessed to have our family reunion. During this time, a few of my family members researched our family history and discovered some interesting facts. For years our reunion was the Currie Lane Whitted Family Reunion and for years we continued forward; however, it was this year that the family voted to reduce the name to the Currie Reunion. There were so many connections, and even a few of the past ancestors that had two families. Although the discussions during the reunion began to boil emotions, the younger generations appreciated uncovering the historical background of their family tree. What about you? Continue to roll out the red carpet, inviting the one who has been missing all these years to come with a family history with many connecting ancestorial channels. Who we are and where we minister from has a blood line that reaches beyond mother and father, grandmother and grandfather. What makes the preacher tick the way he or she ticks? The authentic you is now on your way back with a historical blood line that could be connected to kings, queens, warriors, emperors, and you owe it to yourself to research your family history. It's a part of you and it is you!

Your Spiritual Theological Foundations

By this point in the book, we can now see that we are, through asking ourselves these questions, rolling out the red carpet for the soon coming authentic you. I should rename this chapter the Red Carpet Treatment! As we look to minister from the authentic being, we should carefully and strongly consider how our personal spiritual or theological views have been shaped. What influences or who influenced your spiritual views? Growing up in the Church of God in Christ (COGIC), my spiritual and theological views were for the most part shaped through denominational views. How I viewed women in ministry, the holiness codes, the music, even the structure of the services were all shaped through the denominational culture. What is your view of doctrine, spirituality? How do you view God and how do you relate to God?

As I mentioned earlier in this book, my mother remarried when I was about 12 years old and it was then that I would experience denominational transition from COGIC into the Baptist Church. The style of worship was different and the music was different, although the human dynamics were quite similar with slight differences. The adjustment was challenging, but again the Lord had angels in place who would prove to be pivotal in my spiritual rooting and development. One of the people in my early life was Bishop Otis Alexander; I can remember to this day some of his sermons. Aother would be Mrs. Whitman, who served as my Sunday School teacher at New Hope Baptist Church. She was such a kind and graceful woman, and she took teaching the lessons seriously. Even though we were only teenagers, she treated us like we were the most important students in the world. I love teaching and attending Sunday School to this day because of Mrs. Whitman!

What are your spiritual foundations today, and have they withstood the tests and challenges beyond denominations or faith communities? It can stretch one spiritually and theologically;

however, you owe it to yourself to truly ask why you believe what you believe and why you believe the way you believe. Is it your authentic faith, or is it the belief system ingrained in you because is what grandma and others believed? Again, as the red carpet is rolling out there are theological snags that could trip up the authentic you from truly stretching out and walking back into your living.

Show Me the Money!

There was a movie back in the day with Tom Cruise and Cuba Gooding Jr. called *Jerry McGuire*. Tom Cruise plays a sports agent, and in order for him to sign Cuban Gooding as his client he has to "Show me the money!!" In other words, the client was not going to sign a contract if the money was not close to what he thought he was worth. It is time for the authentic you to be shown the money. What do I mean by this? Simply put, where is your money? How do you think financially, and what have you been taught concerning finances? I know for myself, finances were never discussed unless it related to child support, past due bills, money owed, or the lack there of. There are several scriptural references concerning financial integrity and stewardship. One could ask how authentic ministry is if there is no sound stewardship financially. Of course, ministry can not only become more authentic, but I am sure it will definitely become less stressful. If you had parents, guardians, or other relatives that took the time to develop and educate you financially, then that is truly a blessing. Ensure you pass it on to the next generation; as authentic servants, stewardship should be a part of our ministry.

Let's Talk About Sex

As we journey through a few more questions of reflections and journaling, how were you introduced into and what shaped your personal sexuality? It may not have been the most positive introduction, and for some could have been heart wrenching to just explore it even today. This is your journey, and if now is not the time, then don't let this read force you into it. However, sooner or later, God is right there with you and waiting for you to reframe the negative influences on and in your personal sexuality. In some of the contexts of ministry I have experienced, sex has been left off the list of sermons, discussions, Bible Studies and convocations. My wife and I were facilitating a youth conference, and the pastor called us into the office and noted to us that we could discuss anything but "sex"! Of course, being we were the guests and wanted to respect the pastor's wishes, we did not entertain the subject. However, the youth kept asking questions about sex and the struggles they were experiencing, and we were bound by a gag order to not discuss it.

Looking back on the lives of those who were there at the time, some of their marriages later ended. You could see some struggling with their sexuality and could see the direct effects of that on the ministry. When you think of your personal human sexuality, what is your view of it.? Again, not to come with a spiritual agenda in this book; I would only invite you to begin journaling with your sexual experiences, the positive and negative experiences. If you consider your personal sexuality to be unhealthy, then what will it take to get to a healthy place? What does Scripture provide concerning healthy sexuality? Let me add that in my humble opinion, married individuals are not the only ones that the Lord desires to possess healthy personal sexuality. In addition, one's sexuality is not to be ignored simply because they are single, widowed. or divorced, IJS!

Consider evaluating or reflecting on your sexuality and how you view it today. What was your introduction or who introduced you or when were you introduced into your personal sexuality? What was the experience and how does it affect your current ability to be fully intimate or even enjoy the experience? Depending upon your current view of your personal sexuality, it could have a positive or negative affect on your current relationships. There are several instances today where leaders are falling into sexual scandal, addictions, pornography, adultery, clergy sexual abuse, and by the way it is live and spread through live sound and video feeds due to social media. This is why it is important to carry a perpetual awareness of personal sexuality and urges or impulses you may be challenged with. For those leaders with emphasis on clergy, being this book is focused on them, if you find yourself hiding these areas of your life from your spouse or significant other, you may need to consider therapy, counseling, or confiding in an accountability partner.

To confront any building anxiety, we should consider that all of us have dealt with some area of vulnerability while serving in ministry, and there is always an area we are struggling in. It may be a struggle with stress, burnout, obesity, depression, suicidal thoughts, marital, health, mental, psychological, emotional, or simply ministry challenges. No matter what, we all have, are and will experience challenges. This is evident because we are all human. Come on say it with me, "I am Human!" The grace piece of this is that Jesus was fully human and yet all Divine, while we are fully human carrying out a divine calling and vocation. I enjoin you to write that down on a piece of paper or card and carry it with you at all times. At those moments when you are struggling and thinking you are a failure, pull out the card to remind you that "I am Human." As you have reflected upon your humanity and your personal sexuality, let's now look at how that could possibly be or is impacting your relationships.

Relational Reflection (R&R)

The next question for consideration is, how I am relationally balanced? How do I value relationships? There are several contributing factors impacting our relational values. Peter Mosgofian and George Ohlschlager note that there are struggles within us as humans relationally at times due to the "...broken self" [1]. Are there areas of your life or past experiences that have left you broken? Is this currently impacting your relationships? Depending on your current status, this could be bifurcated. In other words, if you are single, divorced, widowed, or separated there could be areas of brokenness steering your relational values, approaches, rejections within relationships. If you are setting the stage to roll out the red carpet to invite the authentic you back in, then you have to invite all of you back; how you relate to others and how they relate to and with you matters. How do you relate to the opposite sex? Mosgofian and Olschlager note that we have the battle of the sexes due to the fall back in Genesis. As a result of this fall the blame game has continued, the tension remains, and if we are not careful we will get stuck relationally in the fallen, broken state Mosgofian and Olschlager speak of. Again, ask yourself how you relate to, serve in ministry with, lead, or interact with the opposite sex and why. If it is negative, oppressive, or aggressive, then you may need to consider actions to address those issues. Please ensure we don't over spiritualize or become hyper-spiritual to cover up our relational deficiencies and try to place dehumanizing, oppressive doctrine in efforts to sell it as God's Word or purpose for a male egocentric hierarchy! In my opinion, this is an ungodly agenda used as a smoke screen to cover up our relational disfunction. It takes courage and much self-examination to remain intentional about our relational values.

Careful examination should include our maternal and fraternal relationships. If you carefully examine the scriptures, you will find numerous narratives providing examples of God miraculously developing His most powerful leaders through relationships or those around them. This would include both friends and foes. Throughout travels both in the United States and overseas, I have witnessed good and dysfunctional relationships due to the lack of relationship values. Take this time to reflect, observe, and measure your interactions with different group or even one-on-one interaction. Consider your reaction or interaction with the opposite sex, same sex, older, younger, disabled, members of the LBGTQIA+, those with the same religion, atheists, siblings, children, and any others I may have left out. If you find anxiety, sweating, heart palpitations, or over all stressful reactions, you may have a deficiency or an imbalance with relationship values.

If there are barriers of communication with any of the above diverse communities, genders, or ethnicities, then we are charged, as servants and leaders, to address our deficiencies. Remember, we are embarking upon ministering from the authentic self. This would include authenticity in our approach, our conversation and our connection as well as compassion and empathy without reservation. Take mental note of any barriers of communication and interaction with those whom the Lord has assigned us to. Do you find yourself avoiding those who make you feel uncomfortable or uneasy? All efforts are geared towards breaking down walls of separation due to our misunderstanding and assumptions of others. As a matter of fact, as you journal, remember to build a list of the "others" and barriers inhibiting the true you from engaging in true authentic and relational ministry.

As we get to the final few questions of authentic ministry and discovering the true authentic self, ask yourself without hesitation or reservation: Did I experience vacations, respite, life outside of the faith community? Is the feeling of guilt setting in or is there a feeling of grief or frustration because I have not unplugged? Let's get one thing straight and let's be clear, a church conference, convocation, or religious seminar is not considered vacation. This should be a time to totally unplug from title, resume, degrees, and positions as you escape to just simply be. It is all about existence as who God created you to be. I often share with friends and colleagues that for years I was used to hanging out with Pastor Austin, Dr. Austin, Professor Austin, Reverend Austin; however, I love hanging out with Eugene. When I was born my parents named me Eugene K. Austin II and once I invited Eugene back into the picture and scene of life, I would much rather hang out with him than with the others. For our twenty-fifth wedding anniversary, I scheduled a vacation to Punta Cana, Dominican Republic, and one of the most liberating experiences was landing on the island, checking into the hotel, placing my phone in the room, walking down to the pool, and spending the entire day unplugged from all the titles and demands. It changed my life, blessed my marriage, and upon return from the 10-day vacation, I can truly say the authentic me began to flourish. You would be amazed how blessed those you serve, starting with your immediate family, will be from you unplugging. By the way, I don't remember asking for permission; however, I did notify my supervisor and the obligations I am accountable to and for. It is so much healthier to voluntarily schedule vacation instead of an involuntary, unscheduled time of sick leave due to burnout, stress, or illness. As a matter of fact, it's been five years and we are embarking upon 30 years of marriage and I would say it's about that time again. So again, as you take time to journal, take time to plan out your vacation. Ensure you include cost, dates, place, and even activities. Come on now, what are you waiting on, you know the true "authentic you" needs time off and is waiting to have powerful self-talks. This is a golden opportunity to have a discussion within to share how much you miss the true you, how much you miss being you as God designed, journeying with you and only you as the authentic you. I can see you now, hanging up that robe, putting that cross away, going out and shopping for those shorts, bathing suits, beach shoes, and shades. Come on now, you know you can't wait to get away, and remember, you better not dare schedule your next convention before you schedule your next vacation. Even if you are single, it is no one else's business where you are going, how long you will be gone, or even who is going with you. One last thing: stay off social media or at least try not posting anything. Keep this trip between you, yourself, and God. Feels good, doesn't it? If you are still having reservations about scheduling time for respite, I want to share few statistics from Dr. Eri Scalise's book *Burnout, Stress & Compassion Fatigue: Managing Yourself.* Dr. Scalise provides the following stress factors facing today's ministry leaders, including:

- 40% have had an extramarital affair since entering into ministry
- 50% of spouses felt their mates entering the ministry was destructive to their families
- Over 50% of ministry leaders marriages end in divorce
- 70% do not have a close friend, confidant, or mentor
- 71% continually battle with depression
- 80% spent less than 15 minutes a day seeking God (devotion)
- 80% of adult children of pastors have sought professional help for depression
- 80% of seminary graduates will leave ministry within the first five years
- 80% feel discouraged in their roles (85% for spouses)
- 90% report feeling frequently fatigued on a daily basis
- 90% say their training inadequately prepared them for the realities of ministry
- 100% had a close associate who left the ministry because of burnout, church conflict, or moral failure
- 7,000 churches close their doors every year in the United States

This is not the full list, just a few of the results which Dr. Scalise took from the Barna Research Group. Continuing on without respite or unplugging leaves one bound for disaster spiritually, personally, psychologically, emotionally and even relationally. I pray this list gives all who read this book reason for pause and self-reflection to evaluate the seriousness of what we embark upon and the disastrous results of hiding under the covers of titles, callings, positions, and vocations. God ordained for the true you to evolve, healthy, whole, and balanced.

As we now arrive at our final question of self-evaluation and historic culture, what were the emphases on psychological, emotional, mental intelligence/health? It is refreshing to note in the twenty-first century, especially as a post COVID generation, the emphasis and attention given concerning individual mental and emotional health. As one who serves in ministry and the stresses of serving, whether full time or bi-vocational, you should ensure that at least you have an annual physical by your physician. When was the last time you had blood work, what is a healthy weight recommended for your height, or have you spoken with a therapist? Depending upon your culture, ethnic background or family history, your views of mental health or emotional intelligence may not be so positive. I remember for years I did not schedule an appointment. We are talking over 15 years and I had not visited the doctor or had a physical. Upon digging into my family history, I discovered all of the men in my family experienced prostate cancer and there was family history of diabetes. Again, this takes us back to knowing the authentic self, which includes your family history. Not to share too much of my own story, however, it was upon discovering my family history that I scheduled a colonoscopy, during which the doctor discovered five nodules. Thankfully, they were found early and none were cancerous. So much of ourselves we keep hidden that could cost us our lives. It is a matter of life and death to re-invite the one that has been missing far too long back. All your personal history, your family medical history, ancestors, the family stories and narratives hold the keys to not only a more authentic you but a healthier, holistic whole self. Take time to research your history and have discussions with family members concerning physical, mental, and emotional health history. Remember to journal what you discover and take it to your physician as you schedule your annual physical. Your calling, and those whom God has called you to, deserve and require a healthy and holistic authentic servant.

My personal testimony in reflection was during my second year of seminary. Taking a Minnesota Multiphasic Personality Inventory (MMPI) test turned my entire world upside down.

I remember sitting in the classroom on the campus of Virginia Union University, STVU, in the middle of July, and anxiously awaiting the results from the MMPI we took during the spring semester. Everyone in the class received their results first and the MMPI proctor held my results with a very concerned look on his face. My entire paper was highlighted in yellow. All the results noted suicidal tendencies, risk of burnout, anxiety, stress, and manic depression. The warning signs were all there. After the class was dismissed, my instructor and the proctor had a serious conversation with me and there was great concern for my health and mental state. Of course, during that time I was denying all the signs and was not willing to show any vulnerability, weakness, or transparency. There was no way I could show any sign of vulnerability. Interesting enough it would only be a matter of months before I crashed and burned and it would take two years to recover.

It is important to evaluate where you are spiritually, emotionally, physically, mentally, and psychologically. Take time now to take a mental note of any surveys, evaluations, or personality tests towards discovery of where you are right at this moment. There are even ways of evaluating how you are wired. There were times in my life where I strayed away from marriage counseling, therapy, coaching, physical exams or simply selfcare. I was so busy being busy that I was ignoring my being. The lists from Dr. Scalise provided above paint a clear picture of what can happen when we ignore the warning signs. The one has been missing so long that the authentic self is not in view to be examined, explored, analyzed, evaluated, or even diagnosed. Looking over the last several years and the alarming rate of clergy suicide, we can't afford to live outside of the realities of what is truly going on with us. This is a great time to take a strategic pause and journal thoughts, frustrations, anxieties, hurts, breakthroughs, and accomplishments. Secondly, internalize how these events make you feel physically, emotionally, or holistically. Where are you with it right now and are you free to authentically feel about it or are you restricted by how others you lead, colleagues, and friends expect you to feel?

It's your time, so spend time journaling your thoughts, feelings and then wait to see what God wants to say to you.

As you begin to roll out the red carpet inviting the authentic self back into the picture you want to make sure there are no snags in the carpet of life that will trip up or hinder the purposed self from progressing along the way. One of the snags keeping us from being who God created us to be is the unlimited accessibility of everyone, all the time, anytime, every time into our personal and most intimate spaces. One way to minimize so many opinions, hands', and spirits' intrusions into our lives is to set boundaries, whether it is dealing with our cell phones, social media, email, place of business, our residence or just through conversation. Rabbi Julie S. Schwartz, Temple Emmanu-El, explains how "boundaries make it safe in relationships and lets me know who I am versus who you are. Boundaries allow me to keep being me without merging into who you are." [2] Take back the authority and control of who has access to your life and how much of your space you open up to others. It's okay for you to remain selective of how transparent you are with others and who you decide to share the most intimate areas of yourself with. There are those who add to your life, both positively and negatively. It is time for you to evaluate the extra added weight you are carrying and of that weight, whether emotional or spiritual, how did it get there? Or better yet, who placed it there? I noticed that when I began to limit access without apology, the weight began to be lifted. Setting boundaries is one of the most practical as well as spiritually liberating steps one can take, and yes, it is a snag removed so that which is restricting you can resolve.

[1] Peter Mosgofian and George Olschlager, *Sexual Misconduct in Counseling and Ministry* (Eugene, OR: Wipf & Stock Publishing, 1983), 30

[2] Marie Fortune, *Priestly Ministry and Healthy Boundaries: Freedom Through Boundaries.* (Chicago: The National Organization For Continuing Education of Roman Catholic Clergy, Inc., 1997).

CHAPTER 7
Coming Back, How and When?

Now that you have embraced the empowerment to take back your identity, who you are, whom you have been, and the one God has ordained to become, you are now equipped for the journey back into being authentically you. This is to be done without apology, but so carefully and with all humility. Let's be clear, this is not a license to arrogantly and narcissistically rush the doors plowing down the innocent; however, this is an invitation to carefully but yet boldly step back into your true and alive and living self. There is a balance with re-entry. To address the initial portion of this chapter, the proper time for walking into the authentic self is Now! We should waste no more time living through or for the fulfillment of the dreams of others. This is not to say that we don't support others towards helping them reach their life's goals and objectives, but this should never be at the cost of neglecting the fulfillment of your personal dreams, goals, and objectives. This is another time to pause, reflect, and journal those forgotten and neglected personal goals, dreams, or life ambitions. What has been planted on the inside of you yet you have not watered the deeply planted goals you once had? Begin to reflect on that job, that house, the vacation you once dreamed of going on. Remember, this is inside the authentic you. Time to brush off all of the dusty residue piled on top of what you desire and what you have always dreamed of. Go on and go after it.

How do you go about it? Great tools are available today in the numerous applications easily accessible through your computer, mobile devices, or iPads. I have become quite familiar with google tools such as calendar, google meet, and google docs so that as I travel I can keep abreast with my tight schedule and update working documents, minimizing the stress of trying to balance all with ease. Ensure that you are honest with the schedule that you set for yourself. I have included all of my events such as meetings with students, my travel for my corporate job, time with my wife and family, and most important, me time. Me time includes devotion, physical fitness, and meditation. If it is not in writing it does not exist. Schedule it and stick to it. This will ensure you are accountable to your schedule as well as keeping others accountable not to intrude into your life. Again, this is how our identity was stolen in the first place. As discussed in an earlier chapter, setting a schedule is a powerful boundary. As I have grown, I appreciate this term more and more. Come on say it with me: Boundary!

Arriving back to our authentic selves is a process. It is much like catching a flight. You have to go through all the security check points, ensuring you don't get on the plane with anything that could harm you or anyone else along the way. What are some things, thoughts, premonitions, assumptions or misconceptions that you need to leave on this side of the journey? As I have traveled many times by plane, I remember that there may be turbulence along the way. It won't be easy; however, the seat belt sign is on and the captain has come on the intercom instructing you to buckle up and put all electronic devices on airplane mode, trays up. Don't be alarmed; there will be a time when you can get up and move around the cabin, but for now let God pilot you to the next destination. There is a brand-new life awaiting you! It has a sign as you embark off the flight with your name in all CAPS greeting the God-ordained self.

As a professor for Jakes Divinity School, I remember getting off the plane at DFW Airport and there was a driver assigned to me that met me in baggage claim. He was holding a sign in all CAPS reading "Dr. Austin"! I went to retrieve my bags and the driver instructed me to go out to the black on black sports utility vehicle. He settled me in the back seat and he then carried all of my bags out, placing them gently in the trunk. Wow! All of my baggage was safely retrieved, at least that which was needed for the trip. What does this say to the readers of this book? Get comfortable and buckle up for the ride. God has all of your baggage pulled off and claimed. That which is needed for this journey will be ready when needed. As I sit and write this book, I am just excited to see what awaits your next chapter as you minister out of who the Lord ordained you to be versus who others required you to be.

Speaking of accountability as it relates to scheduling events as a boundary and applying boundaries to keep all accountable, it helps as well to have an accountability partner. Accountability partners are individuals in your life with whom you set agreement in writing to hold each other or yourself accountable to a standard of ethics, set goals, or objectives you have identified in your life. There are accountability agreements that you can develop so that it is clear to all parties what is expected and they will clearly identify roles and responsibilities. I have identified a few accountability partners in my life that are empowered to provide critique, guidance, and advice. These are trusted agents who are invited into my life at a level that others are not privy to. These are individuals I trust. I take pause in this book to thank each of my accountability partners who have spoken powerfully into my life. It is because of you that I have attained several accomplishments in my life. Thanks for loving me enough to tell me the truth no matter how much it hurt at the time.

You can request accountability partner agreements at 4theolf@gmail.com. This can assist as a template to steer efforts towards the development of an agreement between you and your trusted agent to ensure you reach your life's potential. Again, if you are truly open and honest about reaching into who the Lord ordained you to be, it helps tremendously to have that one who God has divinely designed and assigned to you. It may not be your best friend, but they will more than likely become your best friend as someone who holds you accountable.

CHAPTER 8

Start Anew

Now that we have journeyed through trials, tribulations, and discoveries, we now stretch outward and onward to Start Anew! So what does this look like, what are our reservations or hesitations? What will be lost, and what is gained? Will it outweigh what we will lose? Those are all pondering questions, but for those who desire to move ahead, leading authentically, there awaits a world of those depending on the wonderful gifts, talents, and abilities that have been hidden inside of you for far too long. I want each of you, as readers and champions of this great awakening, to hear the crowds cheering you on like an awaiting family anticipating the birth of the first baby of a brand-new generation. Come on and open up your minds and spiritual ears, hear those who await the arrival of your presence to start anew.

So what does it mean to start anew? One of the terms or definitions I would like to use is to begin over again or to start afresh. Man, I am taken back to the birth of each of our children and even after all the years and each of our children being adults now, the arrival of our granddaughter reminds us all of that fresh smell of a brand new baby. I can only image how refreshing it will be to you and to those you are assigned to, professionally and/or spiritually, when the aroma of the new delivered authentic you arrives. You know, since we are discussing the metaphor of a brand-new baby, understand that starting anew is a huge change for all. The blessing is that your changes and transformation occurs over time as you process, reflect, and journal each level of transformation. However, those who will encounter the new you may not be able to fully understand the new boundaries, limitations, schedule, respite, and respect your starting anew will demand from all. It's like an old, soiled diaper. Everyone knows that it needs changing but the baby, as well as those directly engaged in the changing process, dread the process. But oh, how refreshing it is to all once completed. The stench and stains only last for a while, but again are all part of the process. The challenge will be for the baby in us, that resists the changing process, must also resist the tendency to keep jumping off the table before all the mess covering up our authenticity and uniqueness is wiped clean, and a fresh set of garments is exchanged for that which is soiled, tainted, and causing us irritation. Oh yes, remember just like those who put up with the awful smell of that baby with a soiled diaper, they have for a while tolerated an inauthentic you, not wanting to say anything because it would possibly be offensive and ruin the relationship. Well, this book is God-ordained to do the dirty work and etch out the changing process that so many may have passed up, the opportunity to truthfully inform and empower you to begin the process.

So as we chart out this process and plan to start anew, take this time to do some serious internal digging and journal the areas that truly are soiled and covering up who God ordained you to be. Journal not only where the cleaning needs to be, what needs to be cleaned out and off, but also begin to strategize a methodology to begin the cleaning. Who are the trusted agents and accountability partners that can assist you with building timelines and itemizing a step by step plan towards you starting anew? Again, just as with changing a baby, you don't trust everyone with the changing process. This may be hard, but who are those you trust with sharing this intimate uncovering of possibly some hidden soiled memories and traumatic experiences? As a matter of fact, this is a great time to also include professional resources that you may need to research, such as counselors, therapists, certified life coaches, mentors and even mentees that you trust to serve as active, trusted change agents. Kenneth J. McFayden has a great book entitled *Strategic Leadership for a Change: Facing our Losses, Finding our Future* that discusses strategic change that could be a great resource during this journey. This book comes with a templated journal that makes steering these efforts easier to navigate. It is the Creator's will for you to serve as you. No one can do for God what God has called and created you to do like you can. Surely you have to know by now that He desires you! You have to step forward as only you can. For those who may pick up this book and journey through it who may not so much be Christian, you can still utilize the tools this book employs to search out spiritual leaders, books, therapists, and life coaches or counselors to be the best you there is.

As you continue to journal, begin as well to list those quiet places that are most conducive for meditation, reflection, and strategizing. What is your most productive time of day, or high energy times where you can get the most accomplished? This chapter doesn't have to go too far in depth, being that future templated journals will steer these efforts, so we won't provide too much detail to avoid hijacking this process. This is your journey and the plan that you will develop. As you bring to a close this portion of journaling and you begin to carry out the action steps towards starting anew, you may discover this season of your life will include uncharted territory. It is new discoveries about yourself, how you think, your new routines and the eulogizing of old habits, urges, and living. By the way, this may include dissolving or discontinuing unhealthy, toxic relationships. This may include those who have been slowly chipping away at the true you for years. It may not be easy, but newness awaits you, and as some have said in the past "out with the old, in with the new." When journeying through uncharted territory, remember to pull out a road map so that if you go off course you can return to a familiar and trusted point of reference. As those who are Christians will read this work, what does the Bible provide about not only what God has ordained for you anew, but what tools are biblically offered to ensure we arrive where the Lord has ordained you to be, safely and according to the Lord's plan and in the Spirit of Christ?

Throughout this book you are granted times for reflection, respite, and journaling, so it seems only fitting that you take this time to reflect and record what startng anew looks like externally, internally, physically, psychologically, spiritually, and emotionally. What new discoveries have you uncovered about yourself and others? What are your thoughts concerning your current marital status? Have positive thoughts replaced negative thoughts concerning the fact that you are intentional as we process what has, is, and what may unfold in our lives? We can begin to empower ourselves, taking control of our thoughts and grasping negative thoughts that we won't make it and embracing that we can do "all things" through and in Christ who is our strength. We vow at this time to live life from this point actively in place of the past passive approaches to those areas that have suppressed the wonderfully, beautifully created YOU!

Now that you have arrived at newness and completed inventory of your new discoveries, it is as important for you to take inventory of the tools you will need to continue on this journey. When we talk about these tools, we are referring to those discussed earlier in the book. In other words, what strategies do you have in place to ensure set boundaries are re-enforced? I know for myself personally, the boundaries I have set forth are at times flexed but never broken. There was a time earlier in my career there was unlimited access to my time, resources, talents, and gifts. However, once I experienced broken trust and critical damage that affected my entire family, I recognized that as I climbed higher corporately as well as elevated in ministry, I had to implement safety measures, boundaries, that would ensure the safety of all those I cared for and cherished, and most importantly, me! Remember, you don't have to answer all texts, phone calls, emails, chats, or messenger notifications on demand. One phone call, listening to a voicemail, or responding too quickly to a text can throw off your entire day. It's your day, your phone, your email account, so you may need to set times when you answer emails, texts, or phone calls.

There are a few business rules or standard operating procedures (SOPs) that have ensured my peace and limited emotional roller coaster rides. Here are a few to begin to complete a new inventory:

1. If they did not leave a message, how important was the call to return?

2. Who is in my immediate circle of trust that has unlimited access to my life?

3. Who do I need to remove and/or limit their access to my life?

4. What tools were important during my journey that will not benefit me in the land of anew?

5. What time is my time (Me Time) and what are the rules while I am in this time zone?

6. What is the self inventory of the new me or the authentic me in the land of anew?

This is important to note, the above inventory as well as the things that need to be thrown out at this point in your life. The new you requires new tools, new thinking, new approaches, new responses and a new time table. I recently traveled to the west coast and I found out that the clothing, the shoes, and even the setup of my phone settings changed. That which I needed for my flight, to access the rental car, would soon be discarded before I even boarded my plane to return home. Once I landed back in my home state, there were some changes that were immediately noticed by my family. The person that left just a few days ago has returned, and not only have I changed in some areas that which sustained me while away are no longer needed or effective where I am now. Take this into account as you equip yourself as the newly discovered, God-ordained, divinely called YOU! Much of that which was once critical to where you were in the past has now become a weight. I believe there is a scripture that talks about what we are to do with weights in our lives. Not only is it critical for your new journey but it is also Biblical.

You may find yourself with much more peace and clarity of thinking now that you have began to sift out and through those who have been leaching, draining, and at times even adding toxic contamination in and to your life. If we look at Jesus, the closer He came to the cross the smaller His circle became, to the point that once on the cross He was in between two individuals that He had never met before. Yet the blessing is that even in death the Lord blessed others and it was at the point of death the Lord was transformed into that who even His disciples did not recognize initially. The best part about it was that upon His final assent He would be and is on the right hand of God. Look at your life and notice that the more you uncover the one who has been missing all these years the more you can exhale, now that you areliving closer and more relational with God, without apology and intentional. You don't have to hide any more. You can remain one with the Lord, uncovered and naked as the ordained, comical, creative, gifted, talented, transformational, and divinely purposed blessing to all those you are called to.

Finally, as you have now entered into the land of anew, you have completed inventory and thrown out all the areas that are not required any longer, it's time to take out your pen and paper, your laptop or iPad, and begin to write a letter to yourself expressing how wonderful it is to have you back into the plan of God for the world. Tell yourself how much you missed you, how excited you are for the new journey, the places you have scheduled, the shows you will go see, the lands you will travel to. It could be a love letter to you taking time to tell you how much you love yourself, share the plans you have to take better care of you, make healthier decisions, do more selfcare and maintenance to the most important one in the world...YOU! It's a shame that you have probably written several love letters to others but yet have probably never written a love letter to you. Remember, this is probably because you have been missing in action, MIA, for so long. This can be recorded right in your journal so that you can go back later and reflect on this moment, especially if you go off track and let this fast paced, social media driven world hijack your identity again. This is not a one-time event or decision but is a lifestyle with an agreement and personal covenant that we will from this day forward live intentionally and authentically no matter what.

As it is evident you have made the bold decision to live authentically without apology and intentional, being you have made it this far through this reading, it seems befitting to make an affirmation as a verbal covenant towards the transformational and empowering crossover from living for others and through the eyes of others into your ordained destiny to live as the authentic Self! It is with this affirmation we agree:

Lord, after careful reflection, I now intentionally walk into who You created me to be. I understand that without apology and on purpose You carefully and wonderfully made me with purpose and destiny. In all thanksgiving I proclaim that it is and has always been for me to live in accordance to what You have ordained for my life. Lord, I understand that the steps I am embarking upon won't be easy or without challenges; however, through Your divine wisdom and guidance all of the tools, strategies, boundaries and SOP's are at the ready to be implemented into my life. Every demonic spirit and overbearing bullies waiting to hijack my life are nothing to be compared to the power that lies within me. For I know that greater is in me than any one, thing, spirit or distraction in the world. This is a life style change empowering me at levels I could have ever imagined and I am thankful for the great alarm sounding in my life. God, I am so excited to begin anew with someone who has been missing far too long, and I am excited for new beginnings, discoveries, revelations towards relational, authentic ministry and service. This I affirm over my life this day_____, year_____!

Of course, this affirmation can be tailored to fit your life, profession, ministry or situation. Again, this entire book is arranged and presented from an empowering approach. It is not meant to provide strict, codified, limiting models. I believe there are no one size fits all models. Every reader is unique and special, gifted and talented in their own special way. No matter what changes you need to make to the above affirmation, just promise yourself that you will make an affirmation over your life to welcome with open arms the one missing all these years back into actively living your life.

CHAPTER 9
Making Amends

So now at the cusp of the entire matter of intentionally and willingly inviting the authentic You back into full time living is making amends to all who have been damaged by your absence. Who do we need to make amends to and how will we go about righting the wrong? This must be approached with much care and intentional efforts not to live in the past too long, but long enough to make amends.

Most of those damaged the most or who experienced the most trauma are those who are closest to us. It is the suffering of the emotional response when one has faced an intense event. Most of the time it involves an event that causes stress, threatens, or poses possible harm. As I look back over my life and the continued stress of trying to live out what I thought others required or expected, I caused much trauma and stress to my family. What violence did they experience due to the fact that their father, husband, son, and brother was caught in a web and a spinning wheel of living out a myth? Even while serving in a major denomination as a national officer, there was a certain look, a certain walk that I thought I had to portray. Wow! The guilt that I am feeling even right now as I am finishing up the final chapter of this book... tears are flowing. The urgency to make amends resonates from my heart, pounding and pushing me to do whatever spiritual, practical and principle- based changes and appointments needed to right the wrong.

It is interesting the actions that intentional efforts will move you to take as you walk into the freedom of living the authentic life God ordained for you to live. This is a great opportunity to take a reflective time and moment to journal what appointments, what discussions, date nights, standing appointments need to be pinned in to make amends. Remember, if it is not in writing, it does not exist; it only resides in your mind hidden from the world and partners to hold all accountable to ensure you finish the journey towards the road back into actively living out your authentic life:

Journal:

_____

_____

_____

_____

_____

It feels so freeing to know that the conversations that my wife and I have are now at times detached from religious, denominational, church conferences, events or experiences connected with our positions, titles or church affiliated responsibilities or roles. So refreshing to be able to reflect on the first time we met, looking at a photo of our first date, and laughing at how we missed a major Gospel concert to go hear her sing and win a karaoke contest. Please note that in order for these conversations to remain authentic it must be deemed a safe environment. Let me caution you to be careful what you ask for, because your spouse just may deliver. One of the conversation rules we communicate by is that we must wait until our mate/spouse is finished and agree that we will move on prior to changing the subject. My wife, who is in the final phase of her PhD in psychology, is much better at this than I. Be open to hearing some things that may hurt but yet are probably much needed for a better, more authentic you. I can say that as a man, I often take it personally, but now I look at it as prophetic in that God is using those closest to me to get me where the Lord would have me to be, where I can't possibly get by myself. Let those closest to you give you the conversation and feedback needed to mold the true you.

Open and authentic conversations don't stop with your spouse but also include those who serve over you and who are subordinate to you. It was and still is amazing how much I learn from having conversations with my children. Once I opened up the door for authentic reflection and feedback my children opened up the flood gates. Being this is my second time serving as a senior pastor, we live and learn, and some of the biggest lessons are those that I have gleaned from the feedback provided by my children. I never imagined the hurt and pain that they experienced during my first tenure. All of the pressure of ministry, my mental breakdown, and hiding my frustrations from the public were bleeding all over my family in our private home setting. Again, a moment of tears right now, being that even thirteen years after my awakening I am still pushed with making amends. The moments at the movies, going out bowling, sitting around the house laughing are so refreshing and have taken a turn over the years. This won't be easy at first.

It will be a struggle making amends in new grounds of the unfamiliar. The moments of sharing with my family now are not all filled with tension, frustration, or guilt; I look forward to sharing with my family. You will notice possibly, since every family is different, a new level of openness in the conversations your children have with you. Oh yeah, I take pause to pop my collar because it is so great and liberating to live again as Eugene K. Austin II who just so happens to be serving as a government civil servant, professor, senior pastor, and life coach, but most of all the great, wonderfully, peculiarly and fearfully made unique Me! Not arrogant or narcissictly rooted, but refreshed and sure that I am no longer living under the titles, roles, or admonishments of others but relaxed in an authentic relationship, holistically and spiritually balanced with God and my family.

There are other amends that may need to be made along the way within your extended family, co-workers, co-laborers in the Gospel, and colleagues. However, please remember that making amends will never be at the expense of going back to living up to others' expectations at the cost of living as the authentic self. We have come too far to turn back now. This is a great time to take a pause for journaling and setting the ground rules for authentic conversations, a list of who you need to make amends to, or better yet, how you feel as you schedule and plot out the road towards making amends:

Journal:

_____

_____

_____

_____

_____

Finally, realize that making amends will always have a cost emotionally, spiritually, psychologically, and financially. Ensure you have a holistic budget as you count up the cost of what it is going to take to "Make Amends." Can't remember who noted this, but those "who fail to plan, plan to fail!" We want to live life strategically and not task oriented. This way we can look down the road and measure how successful we have been at re-inviting ourselves back into the picture. Or have we closed the door in our own faces and gone back to living masked, frustrated, stressful, dysfunctional lives, causing more trauma and damage to ourselves, our families, and those who depend on the divine ministry we have all been designed to carry out?

Ensure you finish the amends list for yourself. Schedule the annual doctors appointments, make perpetual or as needed appointments with your therapists, ensure you have vacations set with you and your spouse separate from those with groups, your children, or extended family. Also note that it is most important to have a standing appointment for your personal times of respite and reflection. It would be a shame to make amends with everyone but you. One of the most spiritual moves you can make is to ensure you take care of you first. Yes! This is the season to be all right with you being first. You have been last long enough.

CONCLUSION

As you have read through this book it is with all prayer and hopes, whether you are a CEO, working in the medical field, education, in ministry, nonprofit, self-employed or unemployed, that you will begin to stand tall and walk in the authority God has destined for your life. Life is so short, and I have personally witnessed families lay their loved ones to rest after an unexpected death with much regret of what should have been said, what apologies were never made. So many experiences where it is evident that with the unexpected events unfolding in our lives we have to take advantage of today. I taught a class one time during our virtual Bible study entitled "Don't Wait Too Long Until It is Too Late."

We are all living with the aftereffects of COVID 19, and honestly, we can all use a dose of therapy and counseling. For the first time in a long time as a bi-vocational pastor leading a growing congregation and as a manager for the Department of the Air Force, I had to come to grips with needing therapy to make sense of all that we have experienced over the last three years. This did not just include COVID, but also processing trauma I experienced throughout my childhood, during adulthood as well as possibly post-traumatic stress disorder (PTSD) from my many deployments while serving in the military. Writing this book took so many years, and I know that it was God unfolding and uncovering so much buried inside of me that all needed to be fleshed out to ensure this book would not bleed all over those who the Lord wanted to deliver through their journey. As you close the last page of this book, begin to open up the closed chapters in your life. Go into those rooms and closets of your life that you have neglected all these years.

Hopefully you will take the time to go back through your journals and see where God was speaking to you about areas needing healing to enable a healthy and balanced life physically, mentally, psychologically, and holistically. Who has God assigned you to that their destiny is awaiting your holistic healing? Their empowered life is predicated upon your healing and wholeness. I remember a book I read during my matriculating through graduate school which spoke of the wounded healers of the world who, if not healed holistically, can have a tendency to bleed all over the very ones that they are sent to lead. Unaddressed or undressed wounds can have catastrophic effects on so many. Remember, we are working to invite a new, healed, and whole authentic you back into the forefront of your living. Take a look back over your history, culture, and family dynamics. No matter how great, grand, or challenging your past has been, it's yours, and made you and shaped you into the wonderful being you are today. No matter what, where, or how you are today, you belong to God and the works that the Lord has begun in your life He shall perform until the end.

There are a few tools provided within this reading for your liking, and I hope that as you take the time to go through the exercises you will do them with intentional efforts to get down through all that is covering up your true soul and spirit. Build up a list of resources of therapists, life coaches, financial advisors, even legal services. Make that appointment for your annual physical exam then do a follow up to see how your health has improved once you let the Lord lift the heavy loads of neglected areas of your life. It's amazing the stress that will be lifted as you learn to let some things and people go. There are joys in life. Discover them and make them a part of your life's perpetual battle rhythm. There are sweet spots in life, and it is your time to identify them. Mark them so that when faced with challenges you can go back to the sweet spots that bring you peace and respite. Far too many leaders, as provided earlier in this book, are dying too soon, and the majority of the time it is preventable.

You are honored and appreciated for merely investing in this read. No matter if you are in school, planning to run a marathon, start a business, produce an album, purchase your first home, planning to get married, if you are divorced or widowed, you are called to be only who the Lord created you to be and to protect that area of your life. This is the book for you, and once you have completed the read please pass it on to others as we all enter into a new era of empowerment over the oppression and dehumanization set forth to rob you of you! No more and never again!

[1] Peter Mosgofian and George Olschlager, Sexual Misconduct in Counseling and Ministry (Eugene, OR: Wipf & Stock Publishing, 1983), 30

[2] Marie Fortune, *Priestly Ministry and Healthy Boundaries: Freedom Through Boundaries.* (Chicago: The National Organization For Continuing Education of Roman Catholic Clergy, Inc., 1997).